Table of Contents

INTRODUCTION 1

STEP 1 5
    Plan and Organize Your Thoughts
        Before writing, identify theme, purpose and reader.
        Use only a few major points ordered logically.
        Eliminate redundant words that clutter meaning.
        Use shorter sentences when explaining complex ideas.

STEP 2 9
    Write To The Point Immediately
        Write the theme and the purpose immediately.
        Put Who, What, Where, When, Why, How in the beginning.
        Write to the point especially in sensitive situations.
        The beginning and the end are power spots for ideas.

STEP 3 13
    Write Informally
        Writing informally is not writing conversationally.
        Writing informally means eliminating outdated phrases and using contractions and personal pronouns when appropriate.
        Translate gobbledygook and clearly explain information.
        Identify self-interest areas of the readers to write for maximum understanding.

STEP 4 19
    Use Simple, Concrete Words
        The simple word is often the more specific.
        Writing should be invisible — don't block the communication by using an obscure vocabulary.
        Acronyms and initials should be spelled out initially and not overused.
        Define jargon for the reader.

STEP 5 23
    Use Strong Nouns and Active Verbs
        Strengthen your thought pattern (sentence) by constructing a strong center.
        Use specific nouns to convey exactly what you mean.
        Use active verbs to keep the message moving forward.
        Use passive verbs sparingly and only for special purpose.

STEP 6 27
    Use Short Sentences and Paragraphs
        A sentence should be one thought or two thoughts tied closely together.
        The longest sentence should be no more than 20 to 25 words: three typed lines.
        Sometimes a paragraph can consist of one or two sentences for emphasis of thought.
        Use short paragraphs, six to eight typed lines.

STEP 7 .... *31*
Write in Complete Thoughts
Complete writing gets action.
Be alert to incomplete indicators such as, "It is obvious . . . ." and "I assumed . . . ."
Include the 5 W's and How in everything you write.
Complete documentation saves future work.

STEP 8 .... *35*
Use Clear Sentence Construction
Use grammar rules as a guide but put communication first.
Recognize common writing problems to help you write better sentence construction.
Construct for emphasis to strengthen meaning — power spot at the end of the sentence.
Use transition words to make your writing cohesive.

STEP 9 .... *45*
Develop by Logic
Recognize the faults in logic and eliminate them.
Organize your writing analytically for logical development of ideas.
All writing is designed around a form but may contain all four forms within the whole: narrative, descriptive, expository and argumentative.
To give weight to your reasoning, use the authority techniques: Examples, Statistics and Quotations.

STEP 10 .... *51*
Persuade Through the Positive Approach
To be tactful use positive words; avoid negative words except when necessary.
Construct sentences in a positive way so they do not accuse; discuss the issue, not the person.
Tell the reader what is, not what is not.
Appeal to human needs. People are persuaded and motivated by physical, security, social and esteem needs.

STEP 11 .... *57*
Cut Deadwood
Deadwood blocks the flow of communication.
Get rid of cliches, outdated Old English phrases, redundancies and buzzwords.
Cut excessive prepositional phrases — substitute one word that takes the place of several.
Tight, but complete writing creates clear communication.

STEP 12 .... *61*
Edit and Revise for Professional Polish
All writing can be improved by editing and revising.
There are many correct ways to write the same information.
Editing is cutting the extras from the writing and keeping the same thought pattern.
Revising is reconstructing the information so it is clear to the reader.

APPENDIX A *65*
Key to Step Exercises

APPENDIX B *75*
Fog Index
100 Most Commonly Misspelled Words
Commonly Misused Words
Punctuation and Mechanics
Writing Without Bias

Writing Resources *91*

12 STEPS TO *Clear Writing*

A Concise Guide for Writers and Editors

Leigh F. Stephens, M.A.
Journalism Department
California State University, Sacramento

Published by Creative Communications Associates
P.O. Box 19209
Sacramento, California 95819-0209
(916) 927-3650

Dedicated to my husband, Bob Aldrich

Acknowledgements

I am deeply grateful to Virginia Kidd, Ginny McReynolds and Shirley Biagi for friendship, inspiration and encouragement through our years of writing together.

A special thank you to my supportive colleagues: Dr. Ray Oshiro, Bill Dorman, Lee Nichols, Loree Raetz, Gloria Heidi, Irene Noble, Kit Cullen, Susanne Sommer, Kimberly Smith, Bernie Kelly, Alice Tom, Barbara Stabenfeldt, Kathleen Skinner, Marvin Eslinger, Donna Vercoe, Dru Bagwell, Laurel Lippert and Cari Lyn Vinci. I treasure my family for their love: Reagan Wisham, Lisa Trask, Jonathan Trask, Sean Trask, Jay Wisham, Peter Wisham ... and the memory of my Father, John William "Bill" Fine.

Published by:
Creative Communications Associates
Post Office Box 19209
Sacramento, California
95819-0209 U.S.A.

Editor:
Dr. Jeanne Abbott

Printed by:
T-Comm Business Services,
Sacramento, CA
Kim and Kevin Thompson

Cover Art and Design:
Karen Josephson Design

Manufactured in the United States of America

Copyright © 1990 by Leigh F. Stephens

All rights reserved. No part of this publication may be reproduced, stored in a retrieval system, or transmitted by any form or by any means, electronic, mechanical, photocopying, recording or otherwise, except as may be expressly permitted by the 1976 Copyright Act or in writing by the publisher.

Library of Congress
Cataloging-in-Publication Data
Stephens, Leigh F.
12 Steps to Clear Writing, A Concise Guide for Writers and Editors

1. Business Writing/Editing
2. Journalism Writing/Editing
3. English Language/Reference

Library of Congress Catalogue Card Number: 90-82694

INTRODUCTION

Techniques Of Clear Writing

Today's professional writing is in a tangle, and the problems are rooted in language history and perpetuated by legalese, government red tape and misguided employees. Nevertheless, business actions must be documented, correspondence written and information disseminated to clients and to the public. Effective communications, therefore, are essential in private business, in government and in the mass media.

Why is there such a fog of gobbledygook and confusion that surrounds writing? One of the reasons is because our country's first publications were contracts and legal notices based on old English laws, which have still not been revised. With that background, it is easy to see how "pursuant to," "enclosed herewith," and "in lieu thereof" have gotten a stronghold. Several hundred years of habits are not easily uprooted.

The second direct reason there are confusing writings is the government documentation required for the professional world today. Laws, regulations and policies exist at every step of a program and require multiple copies and redundant information. One cartoon humorously describes the situation. A Moses-like character stands in front of a gathering of people; he is holding two stone tablets — the Ten Commandments. Behind him is a huge pile of stone tablets. He holds out the two tablets and says, "Here are the Commandments . . . and those behind me are the government guidelines that go with them."

Professional people continue to perpetuate the fog because they are tangled in the red tape themselves. When people are hired to do a job, often their predecessors are no longer around. So naturally, when the new employees begin to write reports, articles or letters, they use examples from the files. Mistakes of the past are recycled, and the old, confusing style gets a rebirth.

Fortunately, today there is a consumer campaign that encourages clear contracts, insurance policies and legal decisions. People are better informed because of television and newspapers, and they are taking a more active part in their own business and legal affairs. No longer will a contested contract stand up in court if both parties do not clearly understand the agreement entered.

A landmark *Plain English* law (Chapter 747-1977) for consumer contracts went into effect in New York State in 1978. In short, this historic law stated that all consumer contracts must be in understandable everyday language with headings in logical order. Since then, much has been taking place due to new laws, mass media and *Plain English* leaders like Rudolph Flesch and Robert Gunning who developed the Fog Index.

The *Plain English* idea is infiltrating the writing world, and employees are introducing many clearer formats and styles for all types of writings. People are beginning to understand that if the material isn't clear, the problem could be the inability of the writer to communicate ideas clearly. With this in mind, now is the time to examine your own writing and to determine what kind of communicator you are.

Clear written communication is not an easy task, but certainly it is a goal worth persuing. We must begin to look at the barriers we set up for people when we put words down on paper.

Effective, clear writing techniques include planning thoughts, coming to the point immediately and writing in an informal style when appropriate. It also includes using simple, concrete words; short sentences and paragraphs; developing with logic; and editing deadwood from the writing.

There's a persistent myth that good writers come in the world that way. We're either born with that elusive talent, or we aren't — most people think they fall in the last category. Yet, writing experts tell us that if we can read this material, we can write it!

Clear writing is the result of clear thinking; therefore, organization of ideas is an essential skill in communicating concepts. Many people produce lengthy, obtuse writing, which in turn clouds the meaning. In contrast, professional writing should be action-oriented, accurate, brief and clear. This book is about clear professional communications.

Write to Express Ideas

Often people write to impress others rather than to express ideas, and at the bottom of this is insecurity. We've been taught from the time we were in elementary school to increase our vocabulary, and we've been rewarded for turning in the longest, most complex report. This unfortunate welding in our minds of big words and complex ideas with high intelligence is the villain of clear communications.

Close to reality is the story of the man who apologized to his supervisor for turning in such a long report because, he said, "I didn't have time to write it shorter." Many people have time constraints, deadlines to meet, and little time to rewrite materials; therefore, they stop short of that final polish that professional writers use to clearly communicate. Yet, developing clear writing techniques and using them will eliminate much work on the final product.

Think in terms of using different styles for different purposes. Writing should be invisible. It should be the vehicle that carries thought from writer to reader. A reader should not have to reread and struggle to understand because of lengthy sentence construction, illogical presentation of ideas and deadwood detractors.

The story is told that during World War II, President Franklin D. Roosevelt received a staff recommendation outlining a plan for the protection of coastal cities. The memo stated, in part, "Other areas, whether or not occupied by personnel, may be obscured by terminating the illumination." FDR translated, "He means, turn out the lights."

Author Robert Louis Stevenson said, "Don't write merely to be understood. Write so you cannot possibly be misunderstood."

One of the writer's more difficult tasks is to take a complex concept and translate it into clear, simple information for the reader. Most of us stop just short of this step. Ultimately, clear communication should be our goal.

How We Communicate

Communications as an academic discipline did not develop until the 1960s. Early theorists attempted to describe the human communications process in terms of telephone communications, and numerous models developed. A simple definition of communications is "the process of people sending and receiving information." A sender of information sends a message to a receiver who in turn gives feedback. This cycle usually continues until both parties are satisfied that at least some understanding has taken place.

Unfortunately, written communication lacks immediate feedback, that is, until some confusing policy has been written to hundred of employees and the feedback is confusion. Telephone calls come in, misunderstandings result and more work is needed to clear up the original communication. So one of the more desirable benefits of clearly communicating is less work and more productive action because of clear understanding.

An example of one of those confusing communications is the following directive, which was allegedly issued statewide by a bureau of investigation:

"Fortunately, the message we asked you to disregard was not sent. Thus, we ask that you disregard the message we sent asking you to disregard the last message."

Language Trends

One of the many variables that affects written communications is the language we use to convey our thoughts. Language is a living, changing process just as human beings are. So often people think they learned the "rules" in school, therefore these are set in concrete. This is not so in American English usage. Our language stylebooks yearly reflect the changes we have made by misuse. For example, we misuse a word for a number of years, and it eventually finds its way into the stylebooks as accepted form. "Can not" is now properly "cannot," yet, "alright" used for "all right" is described as a common misspelling. Tomorrow it will probably be the accepted standard.

The idea of clear communications has allowed us to even bend some of the grammar rules such as the split infinitive just used. Language is not black and white; consequently, communication should be the ultimate consideration.

Every new technology introduced, such as computer science, brings a new language with it. Other languages have infiltrated ours because of wars, immigration and explorations. The problem of word usage exists because my understanding of a word's meaning may be different from yours. One scientist was asked to explain what he'd just said in layman's language, but he resisted by saying, "I don't know any layman's language." Jargon can confuse. Words must be carefully selected, defined and arranged for a specific reader.

Another language trend is to shorten sentences; therefore we use less punctuation. We use about one-half the punctuation that was used around the turn of the century because of the change in style now. Mass media and in particular advertisements have had a tremendous impact on language usage and acceptance of misusage. We are living in the time of the *quick message*. People expect their messages in headline design. They want the *bottom line*.

This does not give us license to throw away the rules, though. The rules have served us well, but we must be aware of changes. As one revision of the United Press International (UPI) Stylebook admonished journalists:

"Burro, burrow - A burro is an ass. A burrow is a hole in the ground. As a journalist you are expected to know the difference."

So many levels of considerations have to be used when examining barriers we set up in written communication. The following *12 Steps to Clear Writing* is a powerful guide for transforming fog into successful professional communication.

STEP 1

Plan and Organize Your Thoughts

Many problems occur in writing because we simply sit down and start writing without a plan. From the research we have done, our minds begin to form a framework for the writing. Yet this framework, clearly defined and organized in our own minds, is the step we often skip.

Certainly not much thought went into writing the following instructions on one office bulletin board: "Due to the reorganization, the basement will be on the second floor. Half of the second floor will be on the first floor, but half will remain on the second. The first floor will move to the basement. We suggest you ask for help."

You should be able to write the theme of your writing in one sentence. Everything you write thereafter should directly relate to that one theme. This applies whether you're writing a one-page letter or a 200-page report. For example, a complete theme might be, "This letter explains to the reader that a $300,000 collective suit is being filed, and the claimant's share, if awarded, is one-eighth."

List the major points you're going to cover in the order you plan to present them. In short factual writing, three to five points are about all a reader will retain. Sometimes we fog information by giving the reader too much, yet completeness does not have to clutter. List only what is most important, and what the reader needs to know.

STEP 1 SUMMARY TIPS

Plan and Organize Your Thoughts

1. *Before writing, identify theme, purpose and reader.*
2. *Use only a few major points ordered logically.*
3. *Eliminate redundant words that clutter meaning.*
4. *Use shorter sentences when explaining complex ideas.*

# Step 1 Exercise
Plan and Organize Your Thoughts

The following California Assembly Bill digest is supposed to be written for the person on the street. How would you organize the information and write it in *Plain English* so anyone could understand its legal implications?

Legislative Counsel's Digest

AB No. 214, as introduced, Lehman: Industrial Welfare Commission: mandatory days off.

Existing law provides that the maximum hours of work and the standard conditions of labor fixed by order of the Industrial Welfare Commission shall be the maximum hours of work and the standard conditions of labor for employees, with the employment of any employee for longer hours than those fixed by the order or under conditions of labor prohibited by the order being unlawful.

This bill would permit the Chief of the Division of Labor Law Enforcement to exempt any employer or employees from any mandatory day or days off requirement contained in any order of the Commission, when in his judgment hardship will result.

Vote: majority. Appropriation: no. Fiscal committee: yes.
State-mandated local program: no.

Before writing, identify the Theme, the Purpose and the Reader.

Ask: WHAT IS THIS WRITING ABOUT?

WHAT DO I WANT THIS WRITING TO ACCOMPLISH?

WHO IS GOING TO READ THIS?

Organize AB214:

1. Write the theme in one sentence:

2. Write the purpose in one sentence:

3. The reader(s) is:

4. List the major legal points:

5. Condense the writing to 25 words or less without changing the meaning and include all the legal points:

STEP 2

Write To The Point Immediately

We're trained in school when writing compositions to give the background and then to lead into the point. In today's busy world, this technique needs re-examining. The reader should be able to immediately get the idea — *THIS is the point*. An idea put in the mind of the reader acts as a magnet to draw everything the reader knows about the subject to aid in the communication process.

So don't wait until the second paragraph and surprise the reader with the purpose of your writing. State the purpose in the first or second sentence. This sets up a logical frame for the material to come.

You should also be able to state the purpose of this writing in one sentence. For example, "I want this employee to understand the three kinds of accident coverage and respond immediately with the one coverage he or she wants filed before the next payroll deduction."

This style of starting with the purpose developed from the journalism format for the *Inverted Pyramid*. All the important information is put in the beginning, and the rest fills in the details. Anyone who reads newspapers can quickly grasp this efficient style. The 5 W's — *Who, What, Where, When, Why and How* — are stated at the beginning.

Sometimes people say they intentionally delay the purpose so they can convince the reader before he or she says "no." Yet confusion and ambiguity do not convince a reader. Write to the point.

For example, one form letter designed by a state board of personnel to give the job interviewee the bad news that he or she didn't get the job read like a regular "whodunit." The point, whether the person got the job or not, was hidden in the fourth and last paragraph of the letter. The reader had to wait until the end to find out he/she wasn't hired! The wasted first paragraph read:

> "This is to inform you of the results of the interview process in which you recently participated. The purpose of this process was to provide an opportunity for a group of State Personnel Board managers and staff, representing several divisions, to review, on a general basis, the qualifications of State employees interested in trans-

ferring into vacant Staff Services Analyst/Associate Personnel Analyst positions at the state Personnel Board."

This deadwood beginning is typical of too many letters, memos and short reports. In communications, the first and last information read is the most powerful. Many letters lead into the body with such outdated phrases as "In response to," and "Pursuant to." And endings all sound alike, "Please feel free to contact. . . ."

Don't fall into this ineffectual way of writing. Start those beginnings with the point and with an attention-getter. End with repeating the purpose for which you're writing so you can get some action from your reader. For example:

Dear Ms. Mason:

When we met last week, we talked about combining our efforts on the new shipping project being financed by our mutual parent company.

(BODY)

Call me when you're ready to meet, and meanwhile send me that project report as soon as possible.

Sincerely,

One clever memo writer got around the boring "Effective Immediately... beginning. She began her memo to her co-workers, "Office donations have gotten out of hand. Every time someone gets sick, marries, or moves 'past go' money is collected."

STEP 2 SUMMARY TIPS

Write to the Point Immediately

1. *Write the theme and the purpose immediately.*
2. *Put Who, What, Where, When, Why, How in the beginning.*
3. *Write to the point especially in sensitive situations.*
4. *The beginning and the end are power spots for ideas.*

Step 2 Exercise
Write To The Point Immediately

In the following problems, see if you can come to the point right away. Write the opening sentence for these situations: (A letter or a memo)

- Henry Williams is a professional pest. You have just received his sixth rambling letter concerning misspending of funds by your agency. Your boss has assigned you to cut Henry off for good!

- Marsha Johnson has not been performing well in her job as typist. Her typing is slow and her copy is full of errors. You must write her a memo outlining the problem and pointing out possible solutions. If the situation is not corrected, she'll lose her job.

- A co-worker has just been injured in a traffic accident while driving an agency vehicle. She was not wearing a seat belt. You must write a memo warning your co-workers to wear seat belts.

STEP 3

Write Informally

The *Plain English* campaign is promoting major changes in writing style today. Some experts say "Write as you speak," or "Write conversationally." Yet if you wrote as you spoke, you'd have to write in body language, grunts and half sentences. Listen to the way people talk to each other. Most of the information we get in conversation is from the nonverbal cues others give us.

One expert commenting on the nonverbal aspect of communication says, "Psychological research has shown that when two people communicate, 93 percent of the total impact is transmitted nonverbally, and only 7 percent by the words that are used."

So written communication must be clear, precise and logical or the reader will probably not get the message. Writing is the most difficult way that people relate ideas. A good rule for the writer is to remember Murphy's Law, "Anything that can go wrong will." Anything that can be misunderstood in writing, probably will be by someone reading it. Another major difference between writing and speaking is that when people speak, they often use cliches and are redundant. Don't do this in writing.

Actually what is meant by writing informally is to write completely, as you would explain the information to someone sitting across the desk from you. Informal writing also means using contractions and personal pronouns when appropriate. An informal writing can certainly use "can't" or "won't," and a good writer no longer writes, "This writer believes," but "I believe."

In writing watch these three areas: (1) Get rid of outdated phrases, (2) Get rid of gobbledygook, and (3) Picture a typical reader and slant your information to that reader.

Outmoded phrases should be easy to recognize. Edit everything you write. Don't date yourself by using old-fashioned language. Here are some examples:

Outdated	Plain English
thanking you kindly	thank you
attached please find	Attachments: (2)
this author thinks	(delete)
let me hasten to explain	this explains
in the vaguest of generalities	vaguely
Very respectfully yours,	Sincerely,

The second area to watch is gobbledygook, although it may be more difficult to uproot. There is convincing evidence that we recognize it in others but don't necessarily recognize it in our own writing. Gobbledygook clouds understanding. It is an indirect and round-about way of writing. For example, this foggy version was written in an accident report by the supervisor, then translated by the worker:

Supervisor: "Failure of employee to accurately estimate drawer closure speed for timely removal of digit."

Worker: "When I pushed the file drawer closed, my right thumb got caught in the drawer."

Another example comes from a Department of Labor publication:

"The occupational incidence of the demand change is unlikely to coincide with the occupational profile of those registered at the employment office."

Translation: "The jobs may not fit the people."

Consumer activist Ralph Nader says, "Gobbledygook is a growth industry. Verbal obscurity, gigantic and intertwined sentences, semantic blahs, bureaucratese, and legal esoterics put people to work. There are people who produce gobbledygook, people who interpret gobbledygook, and people hired to help other people adversely affected by insensitive gobbledygook. It's all part of the Gross National Product.... So gobbledygook is not about to become a historic memory. As any exercise that concentrates power and provides employment, it has a certain momentum."

The third area to understand in writing informally is slanting to the reader. This makes our writing "human communications" when we write to the person. When the word "slant" is mentioned, some think this means writing down or up to a reader, but this should not be so. There are many levels of self-interest to identify and communicate so the reader gets maximum understanding.

This is an idea from Aristotle and applies equally to speaking to people. The idea of slanting is to think of a typical reader and write to that reader's self-interest. This way you can reach more people rather than appealing to the few on either end. You should define jargon — the language unique to your field — and then establish commonality with the reader.

People have different emotions, different educations and different experiences. Don't write everything alike. You shouldn't write to one person as you might write to several thousand people, for example, who read a common newsletter. Yet, you should write clearly and informally to everyone. If you were writing a newsletter to several thousand senior citizens (65 years and older), these might be some typical ideas to consider when writing:

Health - Could be declining, limited mobility, use large print.
Money - Retired, fixed income, conservative.
Sex/Gender - Many are females who outlive males.
Housing - Alone, with extended families, or in senior communities.
Education - Women in that generation rarely had a high school
diploma, yet they are life-educated and life-wise.
Social Concerns - Crime conscious because of increasing victimization of the elderly.

This is just a beginning analysis of slant to a particular group, but you get the idea. Always ask, "What's in this writing that will appeal to the interest of the reader(s)?"

STEP 3 SUMMARY TIPS

Write Informally

1. *Writing informally is not writing conversationally.*
2. *Writing informally means eliminating outdated phrases and using contractions and personal pronouns when appropriate.*
3. *Translate gobbledygook and clearly explain information.*
4. *Identify self-interest areas of the readers to write for maximum understanding.*

Step 3 Exercise
Write Informally

PART I

Write the following samples from reports in Plain English:

"As to how they plan on using the funds, it has been made quite clear by the Governor and his people that their ultimate intent is to try to place all highway money into the general fund and force highway needs to compete with all other social demands for money, handling the entire matter through the regular legislative budgeting process."

"Once adopted by the County Office of Education, the final steps in the study would be the development of a strategy to ensure the County Office of Education's ability to implement and maintain the personnel systems on an ongoing basis. Included in this phase will be the training of appropriate personnel staff in classification and compensation methods."

PART II

Slant your information to the individual reader(s). Take one major responsibility of your work and write a brief description of it for:

- YOUR BOSS:

- A MIDDLE-AGED TAXPAYER WHO DOESN'T KNOW WHAT YOU DO:

- HIGH SCHOOL STUDENTS FOR CAREER DAY:

STEP 4

Use Simple, Concrete Words

The masters of the English language have always used simple, precise words to convey the strongest meaning. Mark Twain declared, "The difference between the right word and the nearly right word is the same as that between lightning and the lightning bug."

Simple, specific words are less visible than words of high-level abstraction, and you can use the simple word over and over again without looking repetitive. Unfortunately, we have linked the use of big words to great intelligence, and this can definitely create a problem in communications. There are places to use the long, atypical words of our language, but most of the time the simple words will serve us better.

Remember, writing should be invisible. If you use long, vague words, they can hamper your communications to the reader(s).

To illustrate:

ABSTRACT	CONCRETE
alleviate	ease
feasible	possible
effective	it works
interface	work together
viable	workable
implement	start
indicate	said
consume	eat

Buzzwords are examples of foggy abstraction. Many professional writers have developed this style of language that takes a translator to decipher.

The following is an excerpt from a job announcement from a city personnel department, which was advertising for an Assistant Personnel Director:

"EVALUATION AND SELECTION FACTORS

The principal factors to be evaluated are: pragmatic managerial diagnostic grasp of current issues in public personnel management; sensitivity to the personal and organizational dynamics characteristic of staff/line interaction and executive interface; innovative adaptation of merit system processes to personnel management situations; a disciplined approach to staff utilization, fiscal allocation and monitoring staff performance; highly effective oral and written communicative skills."

Would you know how to apply for this job?

Often good words are overused, so attempt to substitute for some of the worn-out ones such as, "facilitate," "cognizant" and "utilization."

A United States Public Health Service official, Phillip Broughton, wrote a tongue-in-cheek Systematic Buzz Phrase Projector that recommended such killers as "synchronized incremental contingency." Broughton says you can drop such phrases into any report, but the best part about it is that no one will question you, because they can't understand what it means!

Someone translated Little Red Riding Hood into modern day "buzzwords":

"Once upon a point in time, a small person named Little Red Riding Hood initiated plans for the preparation, delivery and transportation of foodstuffs to her grandmother, a senior citizen residing at a place of residence in a forest of indeterminate dimension.

"In the process of implementing this program, her incursion into the forest was in mid-transportation process when it attained interface with an alleged perpetrator. This individual, a wolf, made inquiry as to the whereabouts of Little Red Riding Hood's goal as well as inferring that he was desirous of ascertaining the contents of Little Red Riding Hood's foodstuffs basket, and all that.

"'It would be inappropriate to lie to me,' the wolf said, displaying his huge jaw capability. Sensing that he was a mass of repressed hostility intertwined with acute alienation, she indicated . . . ."

You get the picture!

Another problem with words is the prolific use of acronyms and initials. These should be spelled out when they are first used, with the initials in parenthesis just after them. Then you can refer to them by the initials thereafter. Use them sparingly. Don't assume that the reader knows what the initials mean. This classic example comes from the California Department of Health Services:

"The SHPDA shall submit a Preliminary State Health Plan, containing recommended revisions of the HSPs, to the SHCC for review. The SHCC may require the SHPDA to revise the PSHP prior to its approval as the SHP."

Add to these problems the jargon of each technical and professional field, and it's a wonder readers don't give up. Jargon is the language of a specific field. A word in jargon may mean one thing in common usage and something entirely different in the professional context. Always define jargon when you use it for those not in your field of work.

Jargon	To the Journalist	Common Meaning
copy	content of the writing	duplicate
slug	key words of story	to hit
point	size of type	tip of pointed object
head	headline	brain container
kill	don't run the story	murder
morgue	newspaper library	room for dead bodies

Above all, use vivid, concrete words to convey more meaning to the reader. Abstract words add nothing to your message and clutter the writing. Also, use the authority techniques—Example, Statistics, Quotations—to help the reader "see" what you mean.

STEP 4 SUMMARY TIPS

Use Simple, Concrete Words

1. *The simple word is often the more specific.*
2. *Writing should be invisible — don't block the communication by using an obscure vocabulary.*
3. *Acronyms and initials should be spelled out initially and not overused.*
4. *Define jargon for the reader.*

Step 4 Exercise
Use Simple, Concrete Words

CONDENSE TO ONE WORD:

_____ at this time

_____ under the provision of

_____ take necessary action

_____ in order that

_____ not later than

_____ in view of

_____ in the event that

_____ afford an opportunity

_____ due to the fact that

_____ during the periods when

_____ in lieu therefore

_____ in regard to

_____ it is requested that

SUBSTITUTE A SIMPLER WORD OR WORDS:

_____	inapplicable	_____	erroneous
_____	utilization	_____	institute
_____	alteration	_____	modification
_____	inaugurate	_____	sufficient
_____	beneficial	_____	expedite
_____	optimum	_____	explicit
_____	insufficient	_____	expenditure
_____	ascertain	_____	substantiate

STEP 5

Use Strong Nouns and Active Verbs

Nouns are the subjects about which we write. Along with verbs, they are the center of our language construction. If that center is weak or vague, our writing is weak also.

Essential to the sentence are the basic elements, a subject and verb(s). Subjects are nouns and their substitutes, pronouns. These pronouns are once removed, so make an effort to use strong nouns when possible. When you use pronouns, be sure the reader knows to whom or what the pronoun refers. There is only one understood subject, and that is the pronoun "you." If I said to you, "Run!" ... the "you" subject is understood, therefore it is possible to have only one word, a verb such as "run," that makes a complete simple sentence.

There are four patterns of sentences (thoughts). The classic patterns are listed below, but be aware that you can move the clauses around in any order.

1) SIMPLE SENTENCE - subject/verb
      S   V
   "Jay wrote the report."

2) COMPOUND SENTENCE - subject/verb, and subject/verb
      S   V   S   V
   "Jay wrote the report, and he filed the materials."
(The conjunction joining these two independent clauses can be any one of the simple conjunctions, such as: *and, or, but, so.*)

3) COMPLEX SENTENCE - subject/verb, subject/verb
            S   V   S   V
   "Although Jay wrote the report, he also filed the materials."
(The dependent clause is first, with a comma separating it from the independent clause. If you switch the clauses with the dependent clause last, you omit the comma.)

4) COMPLEX/COMPOUND SENTENCE - subject/verb, subject/verb, and subject/verb

               S   V   S   V

"Although Jay wrote the report, he filed the materials, and

S   V

he completed the project."

(Note that this last pattern is just a combination of the complex and the compound sentences.)

Think of the basis of the sentence, which is the subject and verb as the cake — the foundation. Everything else you add to the sentence gives additional information around that foundation, therefore it can be considered the frosting on the cake. When you begin to edit, that's where you start, with the frosting.

Verbs are probably the most important part of speech. They give meaning to the action or state of being surrounding the subject. One problem area with verbs is writing too often in the passive voice rather than in the active voice.

Write in active voice when possible. This keeps the message moving forward:

A verb is active if the subject performs the action.
Active
Example: "The manager <u>presented</u> the evaluation."

A verb is passive if the subject receives the action.
Passive
Example: "The evaluation <u>was presented</u> by the manager."

The passive verb is a weaker construction and also requires about 30 percent more words. Use a direct and forceful active verb whenever possible.

Think of the nouns as the substance and the verbs as the action. A teenaged boy when asked by his teacher if the word "love" was a noun or a verb replied, "On Friday and Saturday nights it's a verb; the rest of the week it's a noun!"

STEP 5 SUMMARY TIPS

Use Strong Nouns and Active Verbs

1. *Strengthen your thought pattern (sentence) by constructing a strong center.*
2. *Use specific nouns to convey exactly what you mean.*
3. *Use active verbs to keep the message moving forward.*
4. *Use passive verbs sparingly and only for special purpose.*

Step 5 Exercise
Use Strong Nouns and Active Verbs

Change these passive verbs to active:

1. The attorney was allowed a recess by the judge.

2. Long-term contracts are written by the paralegal.

3. Critical reports are often issued by those knowing the least.

4. Flex time can be misused by employees.

5. The BMW was driven by the administrator.

Underline the subject(s) and circle the correct verb that agrees in number (singular or plural) with the subject:

1. Two legislators, with their secretary, (was - were) present.

2. None but the staff (believe - believes) that.

3. Neither the manager nor the analysts (was - were) in the room.

4. The paper for the reports (seem - seems) expensive.

5. Lack of attention and care (cause - causes) rust.

6. The staff, as well as the consultants, (know - knows) the plan.

7. Everyone, including the stenos and typists, (was - were) invited.

8. The report states that one of the problem areas (was - were) taxation.

STEP 6

Use Short Sentences and Paragraphs

The definition of a simple sentence is "a group of words that expresses a complete thought and has a subject and verb." The longest sentence pattern (see Step 5) has three sets of subjects and verbs, but you would only rarely use it. Every person's style of writing is different. You and I might write the same information, and you would write two medium-length sentences, one short and two long. I might write one medium length sentence, two long sentences and one short. *Style is your written personality.*

The best practice is to use shorter sentences more often. This is today's style. Sometimes those who have to write technical material try to cover every nuance and end up with hopelessly long sentences. Particularly if you are writing something difficult to explain, use shorter thoughts to convey your ideas. Remember, you will also create a grammatical problem called a run-on sentence if you keep stringing idea after idea together.

Use short sentences. Practice breaking the writing into more sentences. It is much easier for the reader to comprehend. The reader has time to stop and absorb the meaning before going on.

Especially be aware of readers who do not have your professional background. Write simply and clearly. A long sentence should be no more than 20 to 25 words. Count if necessary. When typing, a good top-limit guide is three typed lines. For example, consider this sentence from a California Energy Commission report:

> "The energy conservation measures undertaken and proposed by the Commission cannot eliminate the need for all of these supply additions, but these programs, if as effective as anticipated, can offset part of this additional need, and thus eliminate some of the economic, environmental and other costs that would otherwise be borne by California residents."

It can be cut in half to this:

> "The Commission's energy conservation measures cannot eliminate all supply needs but can offset additional needs. This will eliminate some economic and environmental costs to California taxpayers."

The same guide for shortness applies to paragraphs. A page with only two paragraphs — long, texty writing — really turns readers away. They are more likely to put it aside to read when they have time, because it looks like such a chore to read. Help readers get the message. Six to eight typed lines are adequate to cover a topic in one paragraph.

For years, journalists have used one or two sentences as a paragraph to emphasize a point. Mass media advertising has had a tremendous effect on this style. Ad copy writers have learned to use the appearance or the format of the message as a persuasive tool. Studies show that the eye is attracted to the material with the most white space around it. In other words, texty materials clutter, crowd and detract from the message.

Master linguist Winston Churchill said, " Just as the sentence contains one idea in all its fullness, so the paragraph should embrace a distinct episode; and as sentences should follow one another in harmonious sequence, so paragraphs must fit onto one another like the automatic couplings of railway carriages."

STEP 6 SUMMARY TIPS

Use Short Sentences and Paragraphs

1. *A sentence should be one thought or two thoughts tied closely together.*
2. *The longest sentence should be no more than 20 to 25 words: three typed lines.*
3. *Sometimes a paragraph can consist of one or two sentences for emphasis of thought.*
4. *Use short paragraphs, six to eight typed lines.*

Step 6 Exercise
Use Short Sentences and Paragraphs

Rewrite the following first page of a newsletter to senior citizens. Break into appropriate sentence and paragraph length. Edit all unnecessary words so the meaning is clear and to the point:

> "In the 'On Guard Special Topic' section of this issue of the bulletin, we have featured an article on the serious problem of medical quackery. The section on cancer cures was prepared for us by Dr. John Bateman, a retired medical doctor who was director of a state department of health in the midwest, and who now devotes part of his retired 'leisure' to assisting the Crime Prevention Unit as a volunteer, particularly in programs relating to prevention of criminal victimization of the elderly. The problem of medical quackery is very serious indeed because fraudulent and deceptive practices in the area of health problems, unlike other forms of consumer fraud, not only have the potential to cheat a victim of his money, but also all too frequently, may cheat victims of health or even life itself. Even though treatment by a medical 'quack' through some miracle cure or device may only be worthless as a treatment method and not actually harmful in its actual effect upon health, it should be remembered that it may still be harmful because its use will usually delay or interfere with swift diagnosis and prompt legitimate treatment in cases of serious or potentially lethal illness."

STEP 7

Write In Complete Thoughts

The purpose of most written material is to get action or to give information. Complete writing gets action. But the message fails unless you've told the reader all he or she needs to know to either act or to make a decision.

There should be a good balance between too much information, which was demonstrated in the previous steps, and not enough information. Much incompleteness comes from writing down the sentences as we would verbalize them. For example:

Incomplete

"The difference was the employees didn't understand the new computer."

Complete

"A problem existed because the employees didn't understand the new computer."

Incompleteness breeds indicator phrases, so the red flag should go up when you begin using phrases such as these:

It should be obvious . . .
Needless to say . . .
I assumed . . .
I thought that he thought that . . .
That is self-explanatory . . .

Those lonely readers are out there somewhere wishing they could talk to the writer, because they're having to fill in the gaps by themselves. Write fully and don't make too many assumptions that the reader knows all about your topic. Every document should stand alone.

To be sure your writing is complete, check to see if you've included the 5 W's and How of the information. One missing element will leave an understanding gap for your reader. Writer Rudyard Kipling said, "I keep six honest serving men, (They taught me all I knew): Their names are What and Why and When, and How and Where and Who."

Adequate research also helps completely cover the topic. Sometimes, just going a step further gives that necessary information that produces the professional writing product. Completely document reports and booklets with dates, locations, principal writers, and carefully keep sources in the files for further references. The good writer keeps in mind that any statistic, quotation or fact used in writing may be requested later. Be thorough; it takes only a little longer and pays in lack of future frustration.

A word should be included about punctuation. A misplaced comma can change the meaning of a group of words, and a comma or other punctuation should not be substituted for words that complete the meaning. Writing with completeness also means writing with precision. The June 12, 1989 issue of *Capitol Weekly* reports on a costly error because of a misplaced comma:

> "The language in California Assembly Bill 839 (about public employee retirement classifications) included employees engaged in 'active firefighting, and fire service prevention.' In this case, the comma followed by the *and* gave the effect of an *or*. This meant that all employees engaged in firefighting or fire service prevention were considered local firefighters rather than employees engaged in both firefighting and fire service prevention. The bottom line is that the payout costs will be 25 to 35 percent higher — millions of dollars."

Sometimes you have been working on a piece of writing for so long that you become blind to the barriers to communication you may be setting up for the reader. You may think what you're explaining is obvious. It's a good idea to write and give it some time to "cool off" before you edit it. Or additionally, have someone else take a look at it. If they get confused at any point, you'd better pay serious attention to changing that part because some reader out there is going to have the same problem.

Now, after that lengthy warning about writing completely, another problem to the other extreme is just as bad. Don't overkill. This edict from the National Park Service of the Interior Department is enough to bore the most detailed reader and invite exceptions to the rule:

> "No person shall prune, cut, carry away, pull up, dig, fell, bore, chop, saw, chip, pick, move, sever, climb, molest, take, break, deface, destroy, set fire to, burn, scorch, carve, paint, mark, or in any manner interfere with, tamper, mutilate, misuse, disturb or damage any tree, shrub, plant, grass, flower, or part thereof . . . ."

Seriously, though, incompleteness causes more work. If material isn't complete, you could be asking for the chore of follow-up writing. Someone should be able to pick up a document 10 or 20 years from now and get the complete ideas. Good writing stands alone.

STEP 7 SUMMARY TIPS

Write in Complete Thoughts

1. *Complete writing gets action.*
2. *Be alert to incomplete indicators such as, "It is obvious . . . ." and "I assumed . . . ."*
3. *Include the 5 W's and How in everything you write.*
4. *Complete documentation saves future work.*

Step 7 Exercise
Write In Complete Thoughts

Rewrite the following sentences so they can be clearly understood:

1. They lost the sale because of a lack of initiative and good salesmanship.

2. He wasn't in at the time but might be later.

3. The difference was the men couldn't complain about the new manager.

4. Enrollment in the course had been low but was now overcrowded.

5. Which make typewriter do you think best?

6. The employees here are paid as well as any other region.

7. I like to write better than Henderson.

8. I think the issues are well thought out, it seems to me.

STEP 8

Use Clear Sentence Construction

English is unique among major languages in its reliance on word order for meaning. Yet, this is the very reason that English is a versatile language. Word order in a sentence is the basis of English grammar. Modifiers must be near the words they change; a prepositional phrase always has the same pattern with the preposition first and then its object, and so forth.

Some rules such as never splitting an infinitive and never ending a sentence with a preposition have somewhat changed with the modern usage process. Mass media have hastened some of the language changes that we used to categorize as errors. For example, this sentence is stronger in emphasis by placing the modifier "definitely" within the infinitive.

"He tried to definitely express the dangers she faced." Sentences written informally occasionally break the rule for not ending a sentence in a preposition:

"Whom do you work with?"

In writing, however, it is best to stick as close to the construction rules of grammar as possible, but remember, clarity and communication of your ideas are the final rules.

There are common problems in sentence construction and if you learn to recognize them, you have developed a valuable skill. Some construction problems are comical and easy to recognize, such as these samples proportedly from insurance claims:

"The pedestrian had no idea which direction to go, so I ran over him."

"I had been driving my car for 40 years when I fell asleep at the wheel and had an accident."

The following typical grammatical problems are good ones to learn to avoid: recognize when you spot their kind.

1. Run-on Sentence
The Apple is one of the best computers on the market, it is so easy to operate and keeps detailed records.

Correct:

The Apple is one of the best computers on the market because it is so easy to operate.

2. Sentence Fragment
In spite of all the preparation for the new system and the additional work by the staff.

Correct:

In spite of all the additional staff preparation and work on the new system, accounts could not be completed by the first of the month.

3. Faulty Pronoun Reference
The committee made extensive plans for the new program, yet it did not discover the inadequacies.

Correct:

After making extensive plans, the committee still did not discover the inadequacies of the new program.

4. Mixed Viewpoint
We all need to improve our writing skills, so you should take a journalism course.

Correct:

You should take a journalism course if you need to improve your writing skills.

5. Disagreement of Subject and Verb(s)
The staff, using all expertise available, were advised of their legal problem.

Correct:

The staff, using all expertise available, was advised of its legal problem.

6. Misplaced Modifier
I loaned the VCR to Bob with the jammed eject button.

Correct:

I loaned Bob the VCR with the jammed eject button.

7. Dangling Modifier
Dangling from the bridge, we watched him turn loose.

Correct:

We watched him turn loose as he dangled from the bridge.

8. **Non-parallel Construction**
The attorney delayed the process and studying the brief cleared the confusion.

Correct:
The attorney delayed the process and studied the brief to clear up the confusion.

9. **Mixed Active and Passive Verbs**
She approached her office, and the doors were opened by a staff member.

Correct:
She approached her office, and a staff member opened the doors.

The way you construct information is your own style. Remember the earlier definition of style: *style is your written personality*. Because you think differently from anyone else, you write differently. There are usually several good and correct ways to write something.

Two writing techniques that will improve your sentence construction are writing for emphasis and writing with clear transition (connective) words.

The most emphatic position for an idea is at the end of a sentence. The next strongest position is at the beginning. The least important idea should be in the middle of the sentence.

Weak:
The state workers cannot be paid until they turn in their per diem forms.

Stronger:
Until the state workers turn in their per diem forms, they cannot be paid.

Writing with clear transitions creates coherence in your writing. Transition words are the thought connectives in writing, and the ones you choose tell the reader exactly what's going on in your mind. Don't overuse transitions though, because then you've created deadwood. A carefully chosen transition makes the writing cohesive: the writing sticks together and the ideas connect.

Here are some examples:

To Show Time
Please send us your offer by this week; *afterwards*, we will look for two other bids.

To Relate Thoughts
Please send us your offer by this week; *naturally*, we will look for two other bids.

SOME TRANSITION WORDS

To Show Time

finally	after
tomorrow	at the same time
then	last
as of today	later
next	while
afterward	before
meanwhile	simultaneously
meantime	earlier
immediately	first, second
presently	following

To Show Results

consequently
so
in effect
as a result
therefore
as this
accordingly
since
in conclusion
additionally

To Relate Thoughts

of course	again
in short	also
that is	and then
at best	besides
naturally	further
above all	furthermore
nearby	last
understandably	likewise
elsewhere	moreover
anyway	next

To Contrast Ideas

but	after all
otherwise	although
in contrast	conversely
rather than	even though
nonetheless	granted
instead of	in spite of
still	on the contrary
however	on the other hand
nevertheless	regardless
yet	notwithstanding

To Compare Ideas

similar
this
as
like
also
again
likewise
as well as
resembling
in the same way

To Summarize

in brief
finally
in brief
in conclusion
in short
in summary
thus
in closing
in review
to summarize

STEP 8 SUMMARY TIPS

Use Clear Sentence Construction

1. *Use grammar rules as a guide but put communication first.*
2. *Recognize common writing problems to help you write better sentence construction.*
3. *Construct for emphasis to strengthen meaning — power spot at the end of the sentence.*
4. *Use transition words to make your writing cohesive.*

Step 8 Exercise
Use Clear Sentence Construction

Correct Faulty Pronoun Reference

Revise the following, making the pronoun references unmistakable:

1. The harder the employees worked on the reports, the further behind they got.

2. State officials say that personnel must adhere to new laws restricting travel claims. They brought them upon themselves.

3. The department had high hopes for a new grant program, but it failed in the planning.

4. Payment will be spread over the time period as soon as the new rules go into effect. This takes approximately five weeks.

5. She will explain how the new member can be oriented to the present system as well as its basic principles.

6. The work can be done during the off season, which takes approximately six days.

7. Several training units are competing with the Advanced Training Center, so they must start their own communications training.

8. When the supervisor read the memo about the man sleeping on the job, he had no alternative but to consider it carefully.

Viewpoint Shift

Correct the following to make a consistent point of view:

1. We all need to improve our reading skills, so you should take speed reading.

2. He sent the memo to all departments, but it was read by very few people.

3. No matter what you believe, one should listen to your employer's opinions.

4. A governor tries to be fair, but sometimes their views are biased.

5. Sit up straight when typing, and you should have your feet on the floor.

6. He wants a promotion, but they don't want to work for it.

7. She worked hard, but poor work habits can hold you back.

8. One must continue to practice if you wish to succeed.

9. One should listen carefully to the children if you want to be a friend.

Correct Dangling Modifiers

Rewrite the following to correct the modifier problem:

1. Dancing and drinking every night, her reputation in the office suffered.

2. Our vacation passed happily, swimming and playing tennis.

3. Hanging from the second story, the crowd watched as the sick man prepared to leap.

4. Having entered his car, the windows were immediately rolled down.

5. Gingerly walking on the cobblestones, her eyes caught sight of a silver coin.

6. To travel in comfort, money is a prerequisite.

7. To get 20 miles to the gallon, moderate speed must be maintained.

8. Having at last reached home, the door closed behind him.

Correct Misplaced Modifiers

Rewrite the following so modifying words clearly refer to the words they change:

1. He knew barely enough to keep the office running smoothly.

2. He only knew accounting and programming.

3. The realignment of power was a whim of his merely.

4. They were told when the crisis was over how close the company had come to bankruptcy.

5. We requested the agency to not do that.

41

6. To be pleasant is one thing to always remember.

7. There are several reasons for the firm's success, among them determination.

8. They, needing to cut down on employees, tried transferring workers to other departments.

9. In past times workers were expected to even when ill, work.

10. I gave my typewriter to Dean with the broken carriage.

Use Clear Transitions

Fill in a logical transition word(s) and transition category:

1. We had waited two hours for the overdue bus;_____, we were tired.

    Category_____

2. We had only three clerks;_____, the volume of mail was difficult to handle.

    Category_____

3. We don't have any openings at present for persons with your qualifications;_____, we may in the future.

    Category_____

4. Please mail us your offer by this Monday;_____, we will seek two other contractors.

    Category_____

5. Thank you for your prompt reply;_____, we don't need any more materials.

    Category_____

6. We appreciate your help in this matter;_____, his ideas never add anything.

   Category_____

7. The department needs your help;_____, the division needs your help.

   Category_____

8. The raise is not effective until June 30;_____, we need your continued cooperation to complete the project.

   Category_____

STEP 9

Develop By Logic

*W*riting objectively is a challenging goal. Much writing that you do should be as free of bias as possible. News articles, legal reports, minutes of meetings, case recordings, and many others require that you write just the objective facts of the situation. Your judgment comes in when you make recommendations, but only after you've proven your point with strong evidence.

Logical writing is orderly, analytical and just common sense. Many variables affect reasoning, and you must take care to put all your information together in orderly fashion. When you reason, you do three things:

1. You collect facts (data), interview for first-hand experience and cite experts and authorities.

2. You reach conclusions from data by inductive reasoning.

3. You apply principles to specific instances by deductive reasoning.

You are most convincing when you use sound reasoning and write this clearly for the reader. The two types of reasoning used to support conclusions are inductive and deductive.

Induction - You use inductive reasoning when you arrive at a new principle from known data.

Deduction - You use deductive reasoning when you show why a specific rule applies to a situation.

Any illogical reasoning is recognizable by the reader; therefore, it is imperative to be careful of fallacies or faults in logic.

The following warning came from a magazine advertisement that was selling whistles to women for self-protection, "If your purse is snatched, push down on this pocket-sized whistle and a piercing blast sounds your SOS call. Carry it in your purse for instant use." So much for logic!

To convince the reader, you must think clearly and logically. Some argumentative writing is unconvincing because there are holes in the logic. Prejudice, unfairness and illogical conclusions are barriers to persuasion.

Check this guide to logical writing:

1. *Clearly separate fact from opinion.* You may state your opinions if they are backed up by facts. For example, take the temperature of a given room. You, George and Ann may go to the thermostat that reads 70 degrees. George says the room is too cold, and Ann says the room is too hot. All three ideas are true, but the thermostat reading is a verifiable fact, and the feelings of George and Ann are their opinions.

2. *Data collection should be reliable and complete.* Gather primary research — straight from the source — interviews with experts, original documents, first-hand studies, observations and others. Secondary research should be the back-up data that affirms the primary research. Check all sides to an issue and do enough research so you are knowledgeable about the topic. Too much research is better than not enough because the reader is rewarded by the added nuances of the well-informed writer.

3. *Don't ignore the question.* When you write around the point, your reader becomes frustrated. Reasons for evading the issue may be insufficient research, data may not be available, or the writer may be fogging the issue to distract the reader. For whatever purpose it is done, it is illogical and a communication barrier.

4. *Don't argue beside the point.* When you ignore the question and deal with side issue, this illogic generally falls into three categories:

   - *Arguing against the person.* Political campaigns are notorious for this one where the character of the opponent is attacked.

   - *Arguing the popular opinion.* "Everybody does it" is not a logical reason for doing whatever it is you're writing about.

   - *Arguing the traditional.* This is mother, apple pie, the flag, our forefathers.... A common business comment that falls into this category is, "It's been done that way for 20 years; why should we change?"

5. *Don't make hasty generalizations.* That means, don't jump to conclusions. "It's common knowledge" statements are the weakest proof you have. Avoid them. Here are a few:

   "All politicians are crooks."

   "Young people are going to the dogs."

   "The lenient court system is causing an increase in crime."

6. *Use analogy for illustration only.* An analogy is comparison and points out similarities between two programs, ideas or the like. Last year's successful project may have similarities to the new project, but saying the new project will succeed as last year's is illogical. Those variables, such as timing may prove this not true.

7. *Use "firsts," superlatives and statistics to illustrate.* Test them against circumstances. Because of media images, our culture worships the "first," the most powerful, the thinnest, the richest, the youngest and so forth. Television commercials sell products constantly by using sports stars, movie stars, news stars to tell us to buy certain products . . . not exactly persuasion by logic. Also, statistics can sometimes be made to prove either side of an issue, so use them carefully.

8. *Avoid the "after this, therefore because of this" fallacy.* One cartoon that illustrates this shows a man walking along the sidewalk. A black cat crosses his path, then a car comes by and splashes mud on the man's suit. The man then kicks the black cat. People want reasons so sometimes they blame whatever is handiest without examining other causal factors. This is illogical.

9. *Don't use nonsequiturs — "it does not follow" statements.* This says B must be true because of A, when actually B does not necessarily follow A. For example:
"The legislator is a Democrat; therefore, he is for the common people." Just because the legislator belongs to the Democratic Party does not mean that he votes on issues for the common people most of the time.

10. *Screen everything for bias.* The word "propaganda" has come to represent biased information. Yet, you are reading biased information right now. This is the author's belief that this is what constitutes good writing. Realize that ultimate objectivity is impossible. People screen information through their own belief system and their own perception of reality. Knowing this makes it necessary to put all writing through the test of logic.

Writing by logic involves examining the total analytical process when developing a writing such as a report. The following process takes the writer from idea to finished writing product. Knowing where you are in the process makes writing easier and makes the information logical and orderly.

Examining the Analytical Process:

1. Identify the problem or topic. Examine the total information and determine what is to be examined or analyzed.

2. Define the purpose of the writing. Do you want action?

3. Locate and limit primary and secondary research. Don't try to cover the world; gather data within limits.

4. Limit the problem by setting criteria for key issues. This will help focus on what to research and develop. Identify criteria for issues such as: management policy, adequate evidence to prove, and financial impact.

5. Outline for logical development. Which pattern of organization will accomplish the purpose of the writing? Some ways to order and outline information include: time, location, impact, title, priority, deadline and cost.

6. Write the rough draft. Determine what is the easiest way to get your thoughts on paper. Everyone has an individual way of doing this. Consider writing your first draft rapidly without editing as you go. You slow the thought process if you get caught up in details. Get something on paper first, then go to the next step.

7. Edit and revise the draft. Make a list of levels to check such as spelling, grammatical construction, organization of outline, and content documentation. Polish that final product until it shines!

Writing types fall into four categories: *narrative, descriptive, expository* and *argumentative*. Choose a writing form for your writing and use the others within it. For example, *narrative* writing usually is chronological, involves people, dialogue and tells a story. An incident report could be framed in narrative writing. *Descriptive* writing is sensory—see, hear, smell, taste, and touch. It is never used as a frame, but as a showing technique within the other type frames.

Expository writing is simply explaining something to the reader. An informational article and a procedure memo are both expository writing. The last type, *argumentative*, is persuasive and is the most biased type of writing. It takes a side of an issue and gives an opinion such as in an editorial or an issue report.Recommendations are argumentative also. The writer tells the reader, "This is the way it is," and the reader may think, "Show me." The writer shows the reader by using the authority techniques. These are examples or anecdotes, statistics or numerical concepts, and quotations or cites. The more controversial the topic, the more authority techniques you need to convince the reader. Show the readers, don't just tell:

Telling
Good writing uses the authority techniques.

Showing by Example
Good writing uses examples, statistics and quotations.

Telling
State taxes are going to be raised next year.

Showing by Statistics
Next year, your state taxes are going to be increased by $248.

Telling
Most experts agree that being completely objective is not possible.

Showing by Quotation
Publisher Henry Luce was quoted in The New York Times as saying,
"Show me a man who claims he is objective, and I'll show you a man with 'illusions'."

STEP 9 SUMMARY TIPS

Develop by Logic

1. *Recognize the faults in logic and eliminate them.*
2. *Organize your writing analytically for logical development of ideas.*
3. *All writing is designed around a form but may contain all four forms within the whole: narrative, descriptive, expository and argumentative.*
4. *To give weight to your reasoning, use the authority techniques: Examples, Statistics and Quotations.*

Step 9 Exercise
Develop By Logic

Analytical writing examines the facts and comes to some conclusion. Following is a format that outlines argument. It is an excellent form for op/ed (opposite the editorial page) articles, recommendations and editorials.

Choose an issue you feel strongly about. Take a pro or con side. Write a one-page argumentative following this format:

1. State a strong thesis (your side of the argument).

2. Give an overview of three supports (reasons) for your opinion.

3. Develop each of your three supports, backing them up with at least one each of the authority techniques: Examples, Statistics and Quotations.

4. Conclude, restating your thesis or paraphrasing it.

STEP 10

Persuade Through The Positive Approach

People are far more receptive to communication if it is delivered with a positive approach. That's an easy task if the purpose of the message is positive, but what if you're writing a letter of complaint — a sensitive situation where tact is needed?

Three techniques for using the positive approach have been developed, and you're more likely to get what you want if you incorporate them in your writing. Advertisers persuade us to buy billions of dollars worth of merchandise a year by using these techniques.

The first technique is using positive words. Some words give us a positive, good feeling and others give us a negative feeling. Even in a negative situation, use positive words and a positive approach. This frees the reader to deal with the problem, not with his or her emotions. How do these words feel?

Positive	Negative
new	negligence
improve	undesirable
encourage	irrelevant
appropriate	allegation
accomplish	blame
benefit	discredit
valuable	eliminate
adequate	terminate
significant	disrupt
assure	difficult

Negative words can cause a reader to deal with negative emotions, and this could cloud the real issues. Therefore, negative words can be a barrier to effective communications. Positive words make us feel good and ease communication.

Take for example this excerpt from a personnel memo that was written to get some correction:

Negative
"Your typing speed is poor and your copy is full of errors. Your work has been continually below office standards. This is to inform you that if you don't shape up, you're going to be terminated."

Positive
"Attached are samples of your recent typing that point out some of the problems we've discussed. It will be beneficial to bring your work up to office standards. I encourage you to improve your speed and reduce your error count through appropriate training and practice. This will assure your position with the company."

A second positive technique is sentence construction. The way you arrange words can also antagonize the reader. Point out the problem, never accuse or blame the person. This blocks the purpose you have in getting that person to correct the problem.

This is the perfect place to use third person viewpoint and use as few personal pronouns (I, you) as possible. That way, personalities are not the focus, and the problem itself is addressed.

Negative
"You failed to turn in the report on time."

Positive
"The report was not turned in on time; will it be ready Friday?"

Negative
"I want to call your attention to the poor work you did on our company's project."

Positive
"The work done on our company's project does not meet the contract specifications."

Another area of positive construction points out that the reader is usually better satisfied with being told what is, rather than what is not:

Negative	Positive
did not remember	forgot
did not pay attention	ignored
did not have confidence in	distrusted
not honest	dishonest
not important	insignificant

The third area of persuasion involves appealing to human needs. If you give people some beneficial reason for doing what you want, you're likely to get action. Think, what is it that will be of value or interest to the reader? One list of human needs commonly used is psychologist Abraham Maslow's Hierarchy of Human Needs.

Maslow theorized that there are five basic needs levels that motivate human beings, and he lists them from the most basic (the strongest needs) to the most complex (the weakest needs). Before a person will move comfortably from a lower to a higher level, the person must satisfy the previous levels. Everyone moves up and down the levels, depending on the perceived need at the time. The following summarizes the Maslow theory:

Level I - Physiological Needs

These needs include survival such as food, shelter, sex and the like. For example, if you're hungry, you're less likely to pay attention to the letter you're trying to complete. The hunger gets in the way of the accomplishment.

Appeal Example:
"Those who arrive on time will be served dinner first."

Level II - Safety and Security Needs

This level involves ourselves and our families, both physically and psychologically. If you're about to be hit by a truck, you don't care who loves you at the time. Your basic need is to get out of the way of that truck. In writing, any appeal that psychologically threatens a person is not likely to motivate them to act positively. Yet, if you assure someone that your suggestion is "safe," you're more likely to persuade.

Appeal Example:
"Completing this project will assure your position in the promotion cycle."

Level III - Social Needs

These needs involve friendship and love — on a one-to-one basis or in groups. We need to belong; we are social animals with egos. For example, in business, appealing to agency pride is a definite motivator if the employee feels a part of the company. "Let's all pull together for the organization."

Appeal Example:
"Your part in this project is invaluable, and the leadership you have provided has pulled us through a tough time."

Level IV - Esteem Needs

Two areas identify these: The feeling of accomplishment after completing a goal, and the praise we receive from others. This ties to Level III in that giving and receiving approval and encouragement are key functions of friendship.

Appeal Example:
"This award is given to you in recognition of your accomplishments."

Level V - Self-Actualization Needs

This is an abstract level and may not be expressed externally except in showing satisfaction. Reaching those peak times when we have our basic needs met and when we feel accomplishment and esteem: this is "self-actualization." Putting all our energies into doing what we do best, and succeeding. Naturally, those times we peak come and go, and we move on to another goal. New needs always arise, and we return to a lower need level.

Appeal Example:
"You are a role model to all women who use their talents to the fullest."

The relevance of Maslow to the positive approach is clear. In order to persuade, find what the other person needs. The lower the level, the stronger the appeal.

STEP 10 SUMMARY TIPS

Persuade Through the Positive Approach

1. *To be tactful use positive words; avoid negative words except when necessary.*
2. *Construct sentences in a positive way so they do not accuse; discuss the issue, not the person.*
3. *Tell the reader what is, not what is not.*
4. *Appeal to human needs. People are persuaded and motivated by physical, security, social and esteem needs.*

Step 10 Exercise
Persuade Through the Positive Approach

Rewrite the following letter and use as many positive words as you can without making the letter sound phony or without losing the purpose for which the letter was written. Use positive construction and appeal to the reader's need to persuade him to do what you want.

Dear Mr. Burton:

I want to call attention to the poor work that your crew did on our department's landscaping project. Here are some of the things I've noticed. We contracted for 50 oleanders; I can find no more than 30. We contracted for low hedge along the driveway; yet, there is none. We contracted for drainage tiles to prevent puddles on the driveway after rain. The driveway is a virtual swamp after the rain.

I can point out at least 10 other deficiencies — and I plan to — when you visit us for a personal look at this work.

Frankly, I'm outraged at what I consider to be an amateurish level of workmanship and the carelessness of your crew. I'm not sure which is worse — the poor supervision or the poor craftsmanship — but together, they've combined to really do us in.

Please call me, and we'll set up a date for you to see for yourself and to take corrective action.

Sincerely,

Dess Gruntled, Supervisor

STEP 11

Cut Deadwood

Overused words are the deadwood of our language. Many of these are outdated legalese, redundancies and cliches. Equally bad are abstract buzzwords that add no clarity to writing. Another offender is jargon — the secret language of the profession.

Deadwood has come about because we cling to word pictures that we feel will convey a quick meaning to the reader. But this type of writing is lazy writing. Be creative and use more of the thousands of words in the English language.

Buzzwords are abstracts that can be used in groups, and they still fog the meaning for the reader. They are vogue words that come in and out of popularity: "the bottom line," "prioritize," "telephonically."

Jargon is the technical language used within professions. Although most use of jargon is to give just the right shade of meaning, those outside the profession many times think it's used as a kind of snobbery to keep outsiders in the dark. Nevertheless, when writing to others, use as little as possible and then define the terms clearly.

Cliches	Better
permit me to say	(Go on and say it.)
needless to say	(Why bother?)
as I see it	(Who else? You're writing it.)
to the best of my knowledge	(As opposed to the worst?)
feel free to	(Assume your reader is free.)

Outdated Old English	Better
pursuant to	about
firstly	first
in lieu thereof	instead
afford an opportunity	give
it is requested that	please

Redundancies	Better
report back	report
the ultimate solution	the solution
a sincere effort	an effort
advance reservations	reservations
a general consensus	a consensus

Buzzwords	Better
the major thrust	the issue
at this point in time	now
as per	about
ongoing	(Isn't everything?)
the state of the art	the newest, the latest

Jargon (Legal)	Better
chattel	personal property
depose	to give testimony
prayer	a request for relief
let	to lease
contiguous	connected

STEP 11 SUMMARY TIPS

Cut Deadwood

1. *Deadwood blocks the flow of communication.*
2. *Get rid of cliches, outdated Old English phrases, redundancies and buzzwords.*
3. *Cut excessive prepositional phrases — substitute one word that takes the place of several.*
4. *Tight, but complete writing creates clear communication.*

Step 11 Exercise
Cut Deadwood

Condense to one word:

_____answer in the affirmative

_____at a later date

_____at the present time

_____despite the fact that

_____due to the fact that

_____for the purpose of

_____for the reason that

_____in accordance with your request

_____in addition

_____inasmuch as

_____in order that

_____in the event that

_____in the nature of

_____in the neighborhood of

_____in the normal course of

_____in the very near future

_____in this connection

_____in this day and age

_____in view of the fact that

_____on the grounds that

_____on the occasion of

_____under the date of

_____with view to

STEP 12

Edit and Revise for Professional Polish

There is a joke among professional writers that if you go through your writing and cross out every other word, you'll have a great style. Yet seriously, anything written can be cut by one-third and possibly by more without changing the meaning, simply by using clear writing techniques as you explain. Writers embrace the concept, "There is no such thing as good writing; only good rewriting."

Don't get emotionally involved with your writing. There is no one way to say anything. All meaning can be constructed just as effectively several ways. If possible, have someone else read your material. Writer H.G. Wells said, "No passion in the world is equal to the passion to alter someone else's draft." So you shouldn't have any trouble finding someone to help.

It is valid to question any point where your editor gets confused. You can count on some reader out there tripping on the same spot. Thank your editor and friend and change the material until it is crystal clear.

Another useful technique is to read your material aloud. Many times you can catch the awkwardness of construction or the omission of vital words.

Editing and revision are slightly different. You edit when you attempt to keep the same writing pattern and cut out the deadwood. Editing is also rearrangement of information, basically using the same words.

You revise when you can't save the pattern. Pull out the information and rewrite it in another, clearer construction. Rewriting is a powerful technique used by the professional writer. That final polish and tightening up of writing makes language an art form. Go through your writing and mercilessly cut out every unnecessary word and phrase. The results will be rewarding.

Unclear

"The Legislature responded to ratepayer protest by introducing bills which attempted to assure the reasonableness of utility planning decisions and strengthen the scrutiny of utility costs which are passed through to ratepayers."

Editing

"The Legislature responded to ratepayer protest by introducing bills that assured reasonable utility planning and strengthened the scrutiny of utility costs."

Revision

"Because of ratepayer protests, the Legislature introduced bills that ensured reasonable planning and examination of utility costs."

Writers spend many years learning to write with simple, concrete words and short, explicit sentences. Be confident enough in your own writing to use these clear writing techniques. Don't write to impress; write to express ideas.

STEP 12 SUMMARY TIPS

Edit and Revise for Professional Polish

1. *All writing can be improved by editing and revising.*
2. *There are many correct ways to write the same information.*
3. *Editing is cutting the extras from the writing and keeping the same thought pattern.*
4. *Revising is reconstructing the information so it is clear to the reader.*

Step 12 Exercise
Edit and Revise for Professional Polish

Revise the following samples from reports:

"With regard to the civil action brought against the facility, it would be inappropriate for the Governor to comment on that action since it is primarily a matter between the county and yourself, and also since it is not apparently pending before the court."

"To the extent that this new distribution of mortgage money is different and more desirable to the Legislature, than what would otherwise have occurred, the agency can be said to have produced a benefit."

APPENDIX A

Key To Step Exercises

Page 6 - STEP 1 EXERCISE - PLAN AND ORGANIZE YOUR THOUGHTS

1. THEME:

AB214 is about an exemption to the California Labor Laws, which are set by the Industrial Welfare Commission.

2. PURPOSE:

This condensation of the original bill is written to explain the legal changes this bill will make if it is passed.

3. READERS:

Average citizens in California who have an interest in the labor laws. Most are either employees or employers.

4. MAJOR LEGAL POINTS:

- The Chief of the Division of Labor Law Enforcement is given the authority to make exemptions.

- Existing labor laws can be exempted if hardship exists.

- California Labor Laws are set by the Industrial Welfare Commission.

5. CONDENSATION:

AB214 permits the Division of Labor Law Enforcement Chief to grant hardship exemptions to mandatory days off set by the Industrial Welfare Commission.

Discussion: What are the communication barriers set up for the reader in the original digest? The first obvious problem lies in the order in which the information is written. If the paragraphs had been switched, we would have gotten the point immediately. The first paragraph is simply existing law, which is background information.

Another problem is the long sentences. The first paragraph is one sentence, 64 words! The legalese doublets (day, days — employer, employees) also contribute excess words to the confusion. Think, since this is about labor laws, if you mention them, you don't need to write employer or employees because both will be affected by this bill.

Page 11 - STEP 2 EXERCISE - WRITE TO THE POINT IMMEDIATELY

Henry:

"Your letters about the excess spending of agency funds have been helpful, but due to the high cost of correspondence, we can no longer respond to letters again on the same subject."

Discussion: If there is a key to Henry's interest, it is that he understands a waste of money, and that could be your appeal to him to stop writing repetitive letters. Professionals complain about getting "pen pals" occasionally, and they can be a great waste of time and energy. Certainly you must be polite and tactful, but you must draw the line when it becomes excessive. It would be helpful in the rest of the letter to repeat what is being done about the budget, and perhaps include the cost of writing an individual letter.

Marsha:

"To bring your work up to office standard so you can retain your job, we are enrolling you in the typing review workshop, April 20."

Discussion: Most government and private businesses verbally warn an employee perhaps one or two times before making a paper documentation for the personnel files. This is the case here. It has finally come to leaving a "paper trail" in case Marsha does not improve. Legally you must protect yourself and your agency, so you have to be very careful what is put in writing. Be positive and mention the real purpose, which is not to discipline Marsha, but to bring her up to par with the office standard. Don't use the negative words given in the situation such as "not well," "slow," "full of errors." Use positive words such as the word "up" in the above example. "Up" is a positive word, but "below standard" is negative. "Retain your job" is positive; "so you won't be fired" is negative.

Seat Belts:

"Driving without a seat belt is illegal and can endanger your life!"

Discussion: Since this is a vital issue, you need to get the attention of your co-workers immediately. The illegality and life endangerment of not wearing seat belts should do that. Everyone probably knows the person who was injured, so it would be best not to mention the person's name in the memo. This would be embarrassing to the person, and reprimanding that individual is not the purpose of the letter. You could say something like, "There has already been an injury."

Page 16 - STEP 3 EXERCISE - WRITE INFORMALLY

Part I

"This administration intends to place highway money in the general fund where highways will have to compete with other social demands."

"The County Office of Education will be able to start and maintain ongoing personnel systems if this study is adopted. The final steps will develop a plan that includes training appropriate personnel staff in classification and compensation methods."

Part II

Boss:

"The contracts I will develop are in communications and will be with government agencies. Some are contracted through interagency agreements and may involve employees from as many as four agencies. The content of the workshops will be writing and editing so the agencies can standardize the materials that come out of their offices."

Middle-Aged Taxpayer:

"I contract with government agencies to train their employees to write clearly so we taxpayers can understand what's happening in government."

High School Students for Career Day:

"I train government employees to write better. I enjoy my work because I meet many new people and get to travel all over the state."

Page 22 - STEP 4 EXERCISE - USE SIMPLE, CONCRETE WORDS

CONDENSE TO ONE WORD:

now	at this time
under	under the provision of
do	take necessary action
so	in order that
by	not later than
since	in view of
if	in the event that
allow	afford an opportunity
because	due to the fact that
while	during the periods when
instead	in lieu therefore
about	in regard to
please	it is requested that

SUBSTITUTE A SIMPLER WORD(S):

invalid	inapplicable	wrong	erroneous
use	utilization	start	institute
change	alteration	change	modification
begin	inaugurate	enough	sufficient
helpful	beneficial	rush	expedite
best	optimum	clear	explicit
lack	insufficient	cost	expenditure
learn	ascertain	prove	substantiate

Page 25 - STEP 5 EXERCISE - USE STRONG NOUNS AND ACTIVE VERBS

Active Voice:

1. The judge allowed the attorney a recess.
2. The paralegal writes long-term contracts.
3. Those knowing the least often issue critical reports.
4. Employees can misuse flex time.
5. The administrator drove the BMW.

Subject and Verb Agreement:

1. legislators were
2. None believes
3. manager/analysts were
4. paper seems
5. Lack causes
6. staff knows
7. Everyone was
8. report states/one was

Page 29 - STEP 6 EXERCISE - USE SHORT SENTENCES AND PARAGRAPHS

Discussion: This first page sample of the newsletter could be divided into two paragraphs. Notice the order of the information as it is revised. It is illogical to begin writing about medical quackery, drop into a little biography of Dr. Bateman, and then go back into the original topic. The biography of the doctor was put in to show his credibility for writing on the subject, so that is why the state of Iowa was added below.

"The 'On Guard Special Topic' features an article on the serious problem of medical quackery. Fraudulent health practices have the potential to cheat a victim of money, health or life itself. Though treatment by a medical 'quack' through some miracle cure may be worthless, it may still be harmful because it delays legitimate treatment.

"This bulletin's article on cancer cures was prepared by Dr. John Bateman, who was director of the Iowa State Department of Health. He now assists the Crime Prevention Unit as a volunteer in the prevention of criminal victimization of the elderly."

Page 33 - STEP 7 EXERCISE - WRITE IN COMPLETE THOUGHTS

1. Poor salesmanship and lack of initiative lost the sale.

2. He wasn't in at the time, but they said he might be in later.

3. It became a problem because the men couldn't complain about the new manager.

4. Enrollment was low, but now the class is overcrowded.

5. Which typewriter do you think is best?

6. The employees here are paid as well as those in any other region.

7. There is nothing wrong with the sentence, "I like to write better than Henderson." The problem occurs when you do not make it clear to the reader whether you mean quality, quantity, competition or enjoyment. If you write, "I like to write more than Henderson." you imply quantity. If you enjoy it, try "I enjoy writing; Henderson does not."

8. The issues are well thought out. (Use qualifiers such as "I think" and "it seems to me" sparingly — they weaken the point you are making.)

Page 39 - STEP 8 EXERCISE - USE CLEAR CONSTRUCTION

Page 39 - Faulty Pronoun Reference

1. The employees got further behind on the reports even though they worked hard on them.

2. State officials say that personnel caused the new travel claim restrictions.

3. The department had high hopes for a new grant program, which failed in the planning.

4. Payment will be spread over five weeks when the new rules go into effect.

5. She will explain how the new member can learn the basic principles of the present system.

6. The work can be done in six days during the off season.

7. Several training units must start their own communications training because they are competing with the Advanced Training Center.

8. The supervisor carefully considered the memo about the man sleeping on the job.

Page 40 - Viewpoint Shift

1. You need to improve your reading skills, so you should take speed reading.

2. He sent the memo to all department, but few people read it.

3. No matter what you believe, you should listen to your employer's opinions.

4. Governors try to be fair, but sometimes their views are biased.

5. Sit up straight when typing, and put your feet on the floor.

6. He wants a promotion, but he doesn't want to work for it.

7. She worked hard, but poor work habits held her back.

8. You must continue to practice if you want to succeed.

9. You should listen carefully if you want to be your children's friend.

Page 40 - Dangling Modifiers

1. Her reputation in the office suffered because she went out dancing and drinking every night.

2. We had fun on our vacation while swimming and playing tennis.

3. The crowd watched as the sick man, hanging from the second story, prepared to leap.

4. When he got into his car, he immediately rolled down the windows.

5. She saw a silver coin as she gingerly walked on the cobblestones.

6. Money is a prerequisite so you can travel in comfort.

7. Moderate speed must be maintained in order to get 20 miles to the gallon.

8. He closed the door behind him when he at last reached home.

Page 41 - Misplaced Modifiers

1. He barely knew enough to keep the office running smoothly.

2. There is nothing wrong with the sentence — *He only knew accounting and programming.* It means he is the only person who knew these things. If you want to say those two things are all he knew, try this: *He knew only accounting and programming.*

3. The realignment of power was merely his whim.

12 Steps to Clear Writing

4. When the crisis was over, they were told how close they had come to bankruptcy.

5. We requested that the agency not do that.

6. Always remember to be pleasant.

7. Determination is among several reasons for the firm's success.

8. They tried transferring workers to other departments because they needed to cut down on employees.

9. In the past, sick workers were expected to work.

10. I gave Dean my typewriter with the broken carriage.

Page 42 - Clear Transitions

1. We had waited two hours for the overdue bus; *naturally*, we were tired. Relate Thought.

2. We had only three clerks; *consequently*, the volume of mail was difficult to handle. Show Results.

3. We don't have any openings at present for persons with your qualifications; *nevertheless*, we may in the future. Contrast Ideas.

4. Please mail us your offer by this Monday; *meanwhile*, we will seek two other contractors. Show Time.

5. Thank you for your prompt reply; *in short*, we don't need any more materials. Summarize.

6. We appreciate your help in this matter; *however*, his ideas never add anything. Contrast Ideas.

7. The department needs your help; *likewise*, the division needs your help. Compare Ideas.

8. The raise is not effective until June 30; *at the same time*, we need your continued cooperation to complete the project. Show Time.

Page 50 - STEP 9 EXERCISE - DEVELOP BY LOGIC

Following is an outline of an argumentative writing, using the given format:

1. *Thesis*: Rancho Seco (a nuclear power plant) should be closed immediately.

2. *Overview*: Three reasons -

   . Millions of dollars of taxpayers' money have been wasted because it is constantly down and under repair.

   . There is no known safe place to dispose of nuclear waste.

   . People who live in the surrounding hundreds of miles around Rancho Seco are endangered because of possible nuclear accidents.

3. *Body of article*: Develop each reason using examples, statistics and quotes from authorities.

4. *Conclusion*: Therefore for the above reasons, Rancho Seco must be shut down for economic and safety reasons that affect millions of people in the surrounding areas.

Page 55 - STEP 10 EXERCISE - PERSUADE THROUGH THE POSITIVE APPROACH

Dear Mr. Burton:

The work done to date on our department's landscaping project does not meet the contract standards. I know you'll want to get the job completed so we can issue payment by April 20, as we agreed to earlier.

Please call this week so we can set an appointment no later than February 24, so we can meet and review the work.

Sincerely,

Page 59 - STEP 11 EXERCISE - CUT DEADWOOD

<u>yes</u>	answer in the affirmative
<u>later</u>	at a later date
<u>now</u>	at the present time
<u>despite</u>	despite the fact that
<u>because</u>	due to the fact that

<u>for</u>	for the purpose of
<u>for</u>	for the reason that
<u>as</u>	in accordance with your request
<u>also</u>	in addition
<u>as</u>	inasmuch as
<u>so</u>	in order that
<u>if</u>	in the event that
<u>about</u>	in the nature of
<u>around</u>	in the neighborhood of
<u>normally</u>	in the normal course of
<u>soon</u>	in the very near future
<u>about</u>	in this connection
<u>today</u>	in this day and age
<u>because</u>	in view of the fact that
<u>because</u>	on the grounds that
<u>on</u>	on the occasion of
<u>by</u>	under the date of
<u>to</u>	with a view to

Page 63 - STEP 12 EXERCISE - EDIT AND REVISE FOR PROFESSIONAL POLISH

"The Governor cannot comment on a civil action that is pending before the court and is primarily a matter between you and the county."

"The agency has produced a benefit because the new distribution of mortgage money is different. This is more desirable to the Legislature than the alternative."

APPENDIX B

Fog Index

There are numerous readability formulas and fog indexes that are useful as guides to test whether writing is within a readable range. After editing and revising to the best of your ability, try this simple formula to see how clear your writing is to the reader.

The higher your score, the less people can read it with understanding. The lower your score, the more people can understand it. A lower score is tied to shorter sentences and shorter words.

Scores between 12 - 18 are at a good readable level. Use the formula to periodically check your writing readability.

1. Count 100 words from a sample writing.   _____

2. Count the number of sentences in the sample.   _____

3. Divide the number of sentences into 100.   _____

4. Count the number of words over seven letters. (Don't count titles or proper names.)   _____

5. Add #3 and #4.   _____

6. Then divide #5 by two.   SCORE = _____

Scores were taken on random samples from the following publications and writers' work.

26	Albert Einstein	14.5	Alice Walker
22	Declaration of Independence	14	*Sunset* Magazine
19	*The Atlantic Monthly*	14	*Esquire*
18	*The New York Times*	13	Ernest Hemingway
18	*The Los Angeles Times*	13	Lillian Hellman
18	*The Sacramento Bee*	12	John Steinbeck
18	*The Honolulu Star Bulletin*	12	Dorothy Parker
16	*Readers Digest*	8	*World* (for children)

100 Commonly Misspelled Words

abundance
accommodate
achievement
admissible
advantageous
affiliate
analyze
appearance
assistance

bankruptcy
believable
benefited
brochure
bureaus

canceled
clientele
commitment
conscientious
conspicuous
correspondent
criticism

deceive
deferred
deficient
delegate
discrepancy

embarrass
eminent
endorsement
enterprise
erroneous
exaggerate
exhibition
extraordinary

feasible

grammar
grievous
guarantee

haphazard
height
hindrance

illegible
illiterate
independence
installation
interfered
irresistible
issuing

judgment
justifiable

knowledge

legitimate
liaison
license

maintenance
maneuver
miscellaneous
misspell

necessity
noticeable
nuisance

occurrence
omission
opponent
ordinance

pamphlet

permissible
possession
precede
preferable
prevalent
procedure

quantity

receipt
receive
recommend
recurrence
relevant
rescind
ridiculous

salable
sensible
separate
simultaneous
specifically
statistics
subsidy
supersede
susceptible

technical
tendency
transferred

unanimous
unique
usable

visible
volume

waiver
Wednesday
whether

Commonly Misused Words

All Ready/Already. The two words mean prepared for. The one word, *already*, means something completed in the past.

All right. There is not a word *alright*. Properly written as two words — *all right*.

All Together/Altogether. The two words mean physically together. The one word, *altogether*, means entirely.

Allusion/Illusion. *Allusion* means a reference to something. *Illusion* means an unreal image or a perception.

Anxious/Eager. *Anxious* means looking forward to something with anxiety. *Eager* means desirably looking forward to something.

Among/Between. Use *between* for two. Use *among* for more than two.

Aware/Conscious. *Aware* means having knowledge or perception of something. *Conscious* means you are not asleep.

Balance/Remainder. *Balance* is a sum of money. *Remainder* means rest of. They are only interchangeable when discussing money.

Bring/Take. *Bring* means come toward the speaker. *Take* means away from the speaker.

Capital/Capitol. *Capital* is the top government city of a state or country. It is also a sum of money. *Capitol* refers to the top government building in the capital city.

Cannot. Through misusage, *can* and *not* have been combined. The preferred usage now is *cannot*.

Can/May. *Can* shows ability to do something. *May* asks permission.

Complement/Compliment. *Complement* means to fit together. *Compliment* is a nice remark.

Disinterested/Uninterested. Now interchangeable.

Each Other/One Another. *Each other* refers to two. *One another* refers to more than two.

Effect/Affect. *Effect* is the result, the noun. *Affect* means to change, the verb.

Etc. Use sparingly or write out, *and others*.

Except/Accept. *Except* means to leave out, to make an exception to. *Accept* means to favorably receive.

Farther/Further. *Farther* implies distance. *Further* implies time or quantity.

However. Better used within a sentence rather than at the beginning.

i.e./e.g. Use sparingly or not at all: *i.e.* means as is. — *e.g.* means for example.

Irregardless. There is no such word. Use *regardless*.

Lay/Lie. *Lay* means to place. We *lie* with our mouth and *lie* down with our body.

Lead/Led. *Lea*d is present tense meaning to guide someone or something. *Led* is past tense meaning having guided in the past.

Less/Few. *Less* refers to quantity — "He has *less* stress than I do." *Few* refers to number — "He has *few* troubles."

Liable/Likely. *Liable* is legally responsible. *Likely* means a tendency toward doing something.

Medal/Metal. *Medal* is an ornament worn on clothing. *Metal* is molten cast iron.

Number/Amount. Both are quantity. *Number* is countable; *amount* is quantity, but not countable — *amount* of sugar in the bowl.

Over/More Than. *Over* is a preposition - "The dog jumped *over* the fence." *More than* is adverbial, "They counted *more than* 50 mistakes."

Principal/Principle. *Principal* means the main, top, most and a sum of money. *Principle* is an underlying rule for something.

Stationary/Stationery. *Stationary* means secure in one place. *Stationery* means paper and envelopes with which we write.

That/Which/Who. *That* and *which* refer to things. *Who* refers to people and animals with names. Use *that* to begin an essential phrase or clause, and use ,(comma) *which* to begin a nonessential phrase or clause.

To/Too/Two. *To* is the preposition — "*to* the store." *Too* is the adverb — "It is *too* hot." *Two* is the number — "There are *two* pens."

Very. Use sparingly. Use strong words, and you won't need it.

Who/Whom. *Who* is used in a subject or nominative position: "*Who* is going?" Whom is used in an object or objective position: "He asked *whom*?" "This is for *whom*?"

Punctuation and Mechanics

The following guide lists common punctuation and mechanics usage. It is by no means a complete stylebook. Those rules that follow are commonly used and misused ones when writing. Look in the bibliography for a complete and current stylebook to keep as a guide at your desk.

PUNCTUATION

PERIOD
1. Use at the end of a declarative sentence.
2. Use for some abbreviations. *The U.S. Department of Energy* . . . .
3. Use to indicate a decimal point. *It cost $24.5 million* . . . .

EXCLAMATION POINT
1. Use at the end of a startling or surprising statement.

    He spent $1,000 on a suit!

QUESTION MARK
1. Use at the end of a question.

    Why is the manager asking so many questions?

COMMA
1. Use after a long introductory clause or phrase.

    After the department secretary prepared the packets, he distributed them to the supervisors.

2. Use after words in a series. The comma before the *and* is now dropped unless it would be confusing to the reader to leave it out.

    They voted on attendance, quorum and membership.

    They voted on attendance, quorum, elections and membership.

    Add to be sure there is no confusion: *When they convened, they voted on what constituted regular attendance, how many made up a quorum, when elections should be held, and what the optimum membership would be for the club.*

3. Use to separate two independent clauses joined by a common conjunction.

Mary brought the donuts, and John made the coffee.

4. Use to separate a nonessential clause, phrase or modifier from the rest of the sentence.

   The president, needing to assure the unity of the group, praised the members for their work in the charity drive.

5. Use to separate modifiers of equal rank.

   It was a bright, sunny day.

6. Use to set off an appositives or aside comments.

   Her mother, the attorney, will be handling all the legal work.

   This is the policy we voted on last year, you may recall.

7. Use after the attribution to introduce a direct quote.

   Professor Sullivan said, "This is the introduction to the lecture on hybrid plants."

8. Use between the city and state.

   We held the convention in Honolulu, Hawaii.

9. Use in dates after the day and after the year.

   On February 14, 1990, he married his childhood sweetheart.

10. Use to set off transitional words.

    *They planned, **however**, to consider all their suggestions.*

    ***Consequently**, the group morale was greatly improved.*

    *The employees worked harder on the project; **as a result**, the work was finished in half the time.*

SEMICOLON

1. Use in place of a common conjunction between two independent clauses.

   George wrote the new report; he also filed the court papers.

2. Use to separate a transition word or words from an independent clause.

   *They were short on postal workers; **therefore**, they could not deliver the mail on time.*

3. Use to separate words in a series that also contain commas.

In taking inventory we discovered we needed the following: staples; typewriter ribbons and erasing tape; paper clips, large and small; 20 lb. bond paper; and double-sided, double-density disks.

COLON

1. Use to introduce a list.

   Pick up the following: potatoes, tomatoes, carrots and wax paper.

2. Use to introduce a subtitle.

   John used the 12 Steps to Clear Writing: A Concise Guide for Writers and Editors as his desk guide when writing.

3. Use to show time if it's not an even hour.

   They will pick us up at 7:30 p.m. for the concert.

4. Use after an independent clause to make a restatement of it for emphasis.

   The city council voted to allow parking: we won the argument after all.

DASH

1. Use after an independent clause to emphasize the last clause or phrase.

   The director announced the winner — it was our manager.

   Marian found the secret of success — hard work.

APOSTROPHE

1. Use to form a contraction.

   He won't cooperate; therefore, we should leave him out.

2. Use to show possession of nouns.

   The man's will power was incredible. (singular noun)

   The workers' enthusiasm came from their positive attitude. (plural noun)

3. Use to show plural of a single letter or numeral.

   We could not believe the A's won!

   Put the 4's in the column.

4. Use to show something has been left out.

   The war was not popular in the '60s.

QUOTATION MARKS

1. Use to enclose direct quotes or dialogue.

   The exact quote from the book is, "Pull the lever forward before starting the motor."

   "Please use the other door," the man said.

2. Use around titles of chapters, sections, article titles, poems, plays, a coined word or phrase (generally the smaller work within a larger one.)

   We read Chapter 5, "The Art of Speaking."

   We read "Progress in Energy Programs," which is Section IV of the yearly report.

   *The teacher assigned an article from **Time Magazine** called, "Purging the Politicians."*

   Joyce wrote a poem she titled, "Freedom from Self."

   The senior class produced the play, "Where Did She Go?"

   He called the odd gadget a "widget."

3. Use quotation marks in relation to other punctuation:

   Put commas and periods inside the quotation marks.

   "Give me a break," he yelled at the umpire.

   The case worker stated, "She was not able to work."

   Put semicolons and colons outside the quotation marks.

   The instructions read, "Remove the cover"; this was obviously a misprint.

   The coach yelled, "Fill in that space": this was his fatal mistake.

   Put questions marks and exclamation points inside or outside the quotations marks, depending on the meaning of the sentence.

   Have you read the poem "Invincible"?

   Susanne asked, "Why must our unit always carry the extra load?"

Dr. Johnson asked, "What was the answer you found in Chapter 4, 'Examining the Peter Principle'?"

The medic yelled, "Move back; give him some air!"

PARENTHESES

1. Use to enclose initials or acronyms after the full title is spelled out.

   The group was called Sacramento Women in the Media (SWIM).

2. Use to cite bibliography sources or laws.

   There were 45,000 cases reported in 1987. (Byron pp. 278)

   The legislators voted on the bill (AB 154) after arguing its advantages and disadvantages.

3. Write out most information. The trend is going away from using parentheses.

ELLIPSIS

1. Use to show omitted words.

   The politician stated, " . . . and those in my district will be rewarded for supporting me."

2. Use to show creative pause.

   The statement made us stop and think about our priorities . . . .

MECHANICS

CAPITALIZATION

1. Titles and proper names of people, locations, religions, races, groups, languages, trademarks, etc. are capitalized.

   Dr. Laurel Dickens, New York City, Russia, Morman, Caucasian,

   Democratic Party, French, Jell-O

2. Capitalize a substitute title.

   The Department of Justice investigates activities of the Mafia.

   The Department indexes those involved in any criminal activity.

3. Capitalize most initials and acronyms.

   The IRS puts out forms for filing taxes.

   WEAVE is an organization that helps women and children escape a violent environment.

4. Capitalize the first word of a sentence and the first word of a direct quotation.

   The minister said, "Honor thy father and thy mother."

ABBREVIATIONS

1. Use periods for most two-letter abbreviations.

   1600 B.C., 4 p.m., U.N., N.Y., 344 W. Elm St. Some exceptions are: *TV, IQ, mpg, mph.*

2. Symbols: Spell out "and," "percent" and "cents." Use $ before the figure for dollars.

3. Don't abbreviate the days of the week, or the month unless it is within a date. (Jan. 3, 1988) March, April, May, June and July are never abbreviated.

4. Courtesy titles—Mr., Mrs., Miss, Ms.—are only used in quotations. Do not use them in articles. Formal titles — Dr., Professor, Gov., Sen., Rev. — are used on first reference and then refered to by the full title on later reference.

   Rev. Mark James led the benediction. The Reverend cited numerous verses from the New Testament.

5. The names of organizations are written out at first reference with the initials in parentheses after the name. Later references use just the initials or acronym.

   The U.S. Department of Health, Education and Welfare (HEW) has had some significant problems in the last few years.

   Congress has now put tighter controls on HEW.

6. States are only abbreviated if used after a city. Never abbreviate Alaska, Hawaii, Idaho, Iowa, Maine, Ohio, Texas or Utah unless you are using them in postal addresses before the zip code.

ITALICS

1. Italicize the titles of books, newspapers, magazines and special long reports.

   The AP Stylebook is an excellent language guide.

   The New York Times is a good newspaper.

   The New Yorker is a quality literary magazine.

   We finally published the *1989 Yearly Consumer Report*.

2. Italicize foreign words or initials.

   Her *c'est la vie* attitude got her through hard times.

   There are several ways it can be done; *e.g.*, collect the materials, sand the wood and then coat lightly with a spray paint.

COMPOUNDS AND HYPHENATION

1. Hyphenate any set of words that you want understood as one unit.

   That is an out-of-date idea.

2. Hyphenate between a prefix if the first word ends in a vowel and the next word begins with a vowel.

   She observed that he was being extra-attentive.

   Or if the second word is capitalized.

   Goldwater can be termed a super-Republican.

3. Prefixes that generally take a hyphen include *all-*, *anti-*, *ex-*, *non-*, and *pro-*. Check the dictionary for exceptions.

4. Use a hyphen to show that a preposition has been omitted.

   The fall-spring cycle was always a consideration in planning.

NUMBERS

1. In writing text, spell out the numbers one through nine. Write numbers 10 and over numerically: 254 members.

   Because there were only five workers, their case loads were approximately 100 each.

2. Use numerals in addresses, ages, clothes size, dates, dimensions, highway numbers, money, numbers, percentages, recipes, speeds, sports, temperatures, time, weights and years.

3. Spell out numbers at the beginning of a sentence, in casual reference (about a hundred), and in fractions of less than one (one-third).

4. Money should be written as such:

   She paid 45 cents for that.

   They paid $1,995 for the computer.

   The teacher spent $49.95 for the book.

   The mayor said he would not spend more than $1.5 million on the project.

5. Use Roman numerals for a person carrying on the family name (John D. Rockefeller III) or for world wars (World War II).

6. Use numerals with suffixes *-nd, -st* and *-th* in these cases: 2nd Congressional District, 1st Infantry Division, 14th Street. (For first through ninth, use words in addresses.)

Writing Without Bias

SEXISM

Sexism is a term used to describe language or attitudes toward a person's gender. It can refer to female or male. Most literature in our American culture is sexist against females in that it has been written from a white male perspective or females have been omitted. Avoiding stereotypes can help avoid sexist language. Do not describe individuals by their clothes, physical description, actions or emotions unless this directly relates to the material you are writing.

In our language, inequality has been perpetuated by the assumption that the white, affluent male is the standard and that everyone else is substandard and needs description. Examine cultural assumptions of the sexes, because they are not true of everyone. Write and speak about people as individuals. You can eliminate most sexist assumptions by testing it by, "Would I write or speak about a white male in the same way?"

AVOID SEXIST TERMINOLOGY

1. Most writing can be rewritten to avoid the "he" reference by substituting a plural subject. For example, *"Members should file their papers by the first of the month."*

2. You can use "men" or "he" when referring to a group of men or single man, or use "women" or "she" when referring to a group of women or a single woman. When the group is mixed, use gender-neutral words: *congressional representative* not congressman, *business professional* not businessman, *newspaper carrier* not paper boy, *the Irish* not Irishman, *humankind* not mankind, *work hours* not man hours.

3. A woman over 18 years of age should be called a woman, not a girl or a lady (This is a class term from the lady and the lord of the manor.) A man over 18 is called a man. Those under 18 years are girls and boys.

Avoid these stereotypical generalizations about women:

1. *Women as mothers of us all. Women as the nurturers.* The madonna, the good girl. All women are not mothers, grandmothers, godmothers, *etc.* Do not assume that all females are caretakers.

2. *Women as the bitch/non-nurturer.* The mean stepmother, aggressive woman, iron maiden, whore, the bad girl, the prostitute, witches, crones, the tom boy.

3. *Women as relatives/appendages of others.* Mother of Mandy, wife of George, daughter

of Henry, sister of the president, the little lady, my ole lady.

4. *Women as sex objects.* Gold digger, seducer, vixen, ripe young thing, babe, chick, sexpot, temptress, charmer, buxom.

5. *Women as housewives.* Little homemaker, keeper of family morals, the cook, the cleaning lady, woman's work. She's wild about detergents, toilet cleaners, floor wax and recipes.

6. *Women as victims.* Helpless females needing rescue by males. Rape victims who "asked for it" by being out at night, by dressing seductively, by refusing sex on a date (a tease), not physically strong enough to protect herself.

7. *Women as brainless.* Woman driver, even a woman could understand this, trying but failing in a *man's* topic — science, math, mechanics, electronics, finances, etc., air head, harebrained, bubblebrain, blonde beauty, shop 'til she drops.

8. *Women as emotional basket cases.* That time of the month, must be PMS, crying, unstable, hysterical, dramatizing.

Avoid these stereotypical generalizations about men:

1. *Men as breadwinners.* The head of the house, the man of the house, the provider, brings home the bacon, makes the living, the decision maker, must make more money than the female.

2. *Men as Rambo.* Macho behavior, corporate raider, political strongman, master criminal, conquering hero, ramrodding executive, unemotional, steel-hearted politician, feels no pain, hard-drinking, loves war and weapons.

3. *Men as insensitive slobs.* Leaving wife and children, assuming he does not stay with or nurture children, Peter Pans (inability to commit), men put work first — relationships second, men don't cry or show emotions.

4. *Men as wimps.* Fags, gays, sissy, mama's boy, househusband, hen-pecked, emotional, going into traditional women's fields: nursing, elementary school teachers, home economics, secretarial work.

5. *Men as lechers.* Dirty ole man, all he thinks of is sex, watches dirty videos/films, reads pornography, you know how men are, somehow implies you cannot leave a female with him safely.

6. *Men as sports heroes/consumers.* Sunday quarterback, sideline hero, all men have a passion for sports, hardhitting, base stealing, game playing, a team player.

7. *Men as car freaks.* Hard driving, mechanical minded, speed demon, spending needed family money for wheels, grease monkey, need sleek autos as phallic extensions.

8. *Men as protectors.* The white knight, saviour, the hero, the prince, superman, superstar, champion, idol, the handyman who can fix anything.

SPECIAL GROUPS

All people belong to special groups, whether because of their race, their age, their nationality, their special interests, their gender, their education, their physical abilities, their intellectual abilities. Bias against groups should be avoided.

1. *Avoid demeaning economic groups.* Domestics, migrant farm workers, sweatshop workers.

2. *Avoid omission.* Not representing the general population in stories is considered racist, sexist, ageist, *etc.*

3. *Avoid highlighting a person's special group* unless it is totally relevant to the story. Do not write "a woman writer" or "a Hispanic writer" as you would not write "a white male writer."

4. *Avoid derogatory words for the disenfranchised.* Outsiders, criminals, suspects, welfare cheats, illegal aliens, drug addicts.

5. *Avoid mentioning age unless it's relevant.* Avoid: "A spry 68-year-old grandmother started the neighborhood safety campaign."

   What has "spry," "68-year-old," and "grandmother" got to do with this woman's civic work? Better: "Violet Johnson of Greenhaven began the safety campaign by circulating a petition among her neighbors. She says she was driven to take action after three burglaries took place on her own street."

6. *Avoid generalizations about any group:*

    All politicians are not crooks.
    All state workers are not lazy.
    All Blacks do not tap dance and have rhythm.
    All Hispanics do not like Chevys.
    All Jewish mothers are not overprotective.
    All Asians are not good in math.
    All Latins are not good lovers.
    All homosexuals do not have AIDS.
    All ministers are not ethical.
    All doctors are not men.
    All single women are not man crazy.
    All disabled people are not helpless.

Writing Resources

Baugh, L. Sue, and others, editors. *Handbook for Business Writing*. Lincolnwood, Ill.: NTC Business Books, 1988. (Letters, memos, reports, proposals, resumes).

Biagi, Shirley. *How to Write & Sell Magazine Articles* (Second Edition). New York: Prentice Hall Press, 1988.

Brooks, Brian S. & James L. Pinson. *Working With Words: A Concise Handbook for Media Writers and Editors*. New York: St. Martin's Press, 1989. (An excellent general style guide).

Cook, Claire Kehrwald. *Line by Line: How to Improve Your Own Writing*. Boston: Houghton Mifflin, 1985. (From The Modern Language Association).

Evans, Glen, editor. *The Complete Guide to Writing Nonfiction*. New York: Harper & Row, 1988. (An anthology for freelance writers, covering writing and publishing for all types of periodicals).

Goldfarb, Ronald L. and James C. Raymond. *Clear Understandings: A Guide to Legal Writing*. New York: Random House, 1982.

Kessler, Lauren and Duncan McDonald. *When Words Collide: A Journalist's Guide to Grammar and Style* (Second Edition). Belmont, CA: Wadsworth Publishing Co., 1988.

Maggio, Rosalie. *The Nonsexist Word Finder: A Dictionary of Gender-Free Usage*. Boston: Beacon Press, 1988.

Murray, Donald. *Writing for Your Readers: Notes on the Writer's Craft from The Boston Globe*. Chester, Connecticut: The Globe Pequot Press, 1983.

Strunk, William Jr. and E.B. White. *The Elements of Style*. New York: Macmillan, Latest Edition.

The AP Stylebook and Libel Manual. New York: The Associated Press, Latest Edition.

Westheimer, Patricia H. and Vicki Townsend Gibbs. *How to Write Like an Executive*. Glenview, Ill.: Scott, Foresman, 1989. (Letters, memos, proposals).

Order Form

For: Book - *12 Steps to Clear Writing, A Concise Guide For Writers and Editors*
and
Laminated *Desktop Guide* to Book

Postal Orders: Creative Communications Associates
Post Office Box 19209
Sacramento, California 95819-0209

Telephone for Information: (916) 927-3650

Please mail only check or money order.

Name _____

Street _____

City _____ State _____ Zip _____

                                                                                                   Total

Send me: _____ copies of **Book:** each $12.95   _____

                _____ **Desktop Guides:** each $3.00   _____

                            CA Residents add 6.75% Sales Tax   _____

                   Shipping $2.50 per Book - $.75 per Guide   _____

                                            Total Enclosed   _____

Allow three to four weeks for processing.
Thank you for your order.